ECONOMICS FOR KIDS
UNDERSTANDING THE BASICS OF AN ECONOMY

ECONOMICS 101 FOR CHILDREN
3RD GRADE SOCIAL STUDIES

BABY PROFESSOR
EDUCATION KIDS

Speedy Publishing LLC

40 E. Main St. #1156

Newark, DE 19711

www.speedypublishing.com

Copyright 2017

In this book, we're going to talk about basic principles behind how the economy works. So, let's get right to it!

WHAT IS AN ECONOMY?

People want to buy things for two reasons—because they need them or because they want them. Within every country and across the world, there are systems for buying and selling. There are also systems for bringing in imports and sending out exports. Goods and services sometimes flow from one country to another. Different types of money and ways to barter exist in every country.

Even in democratic countries, some of the processes related to buying and selling are regulated by the government. All of these activities make up an economy. In summary, the economy of a country is built from the way that products and services are created and exchanged.

Economists study the economy and frequently make forecasts of economic conditions.

A BUSY CITY

WHAT IS A GOOD ECONOMY?

You may have heard your parents or people on the news talking about "the economy." Usually when you hear this, it means they are discussing the economy of the country you live in. When a country's economy is good, there are lots of jobs available that pay a fair wage depending on the skills the worker needs. In a good economy, businesses, both small and large, are making a profit. It also means that the economy has increasing opportunities and growth.

WHAT IS A BAD ECONOMY?

When an economy isn't doing well, the opposite events are happening. There are almost no new jobs and people are being laid off from the jobs they have. Businesses, both small and large, aren't profitable or are closing their doors. Sometimes if the economy is very bad, businesses and people are going bankrupt in record numbers. In a bad economy, there isn't any economic growth.

FREE
SOUP COFFEE & DOUGHNUTS
FOR THE UNEMPLOYED

FREE SOUP
&

UNEMPLOYED MEN WAITING IN LINE
OUTSIDE A FREE SOUP KITCHEN

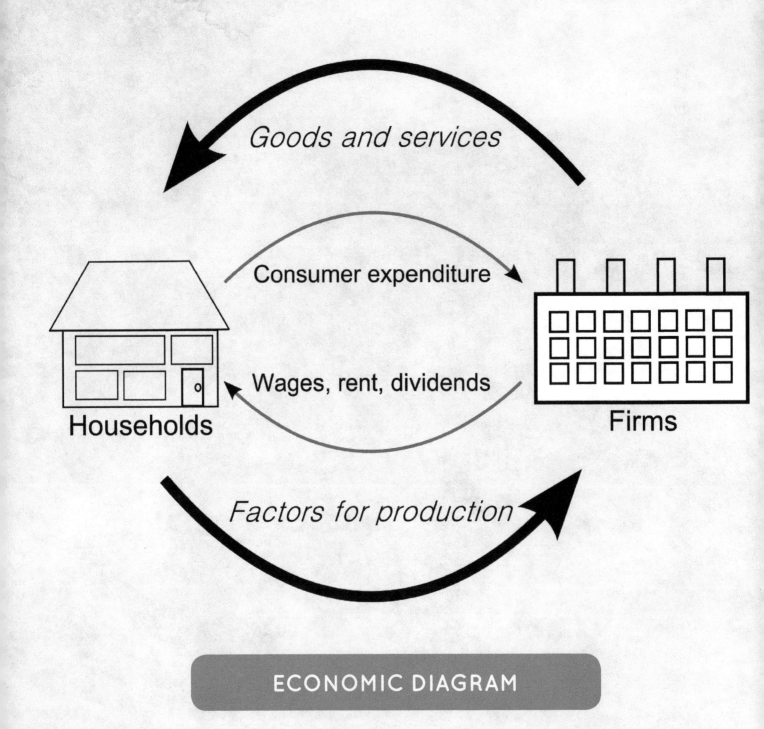

Goods and services

Consumer expenditure

Households

Wages, rent, dividends

Factors for production

Firms

ECONOMIC DIAGRAM

MICRO COMPARED TO MACRO

The economy is a huge subject so economists divide it into two general categories: microeconomics and macroeconomics.

Microeconomics covers how people and businesses make choices. **Macroeconomics** looks at the economy from a larger view.

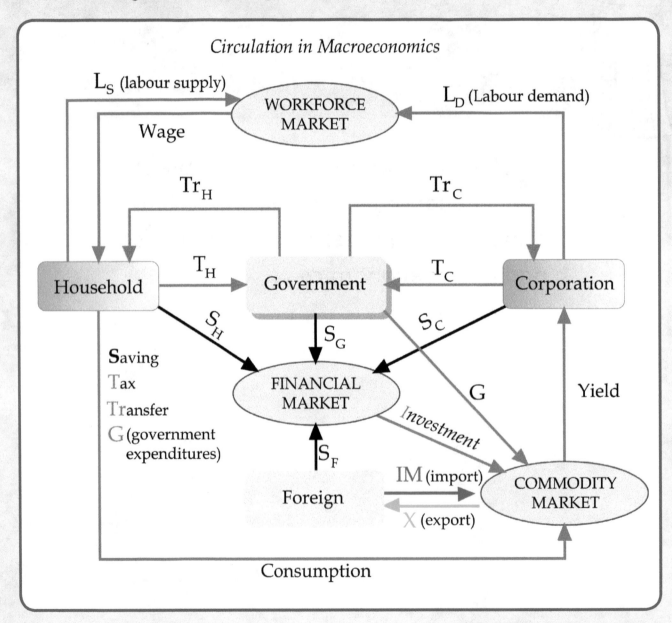

Circulation in Macroeconomics

Economists who study macroeconomics are researching the economy from the national or global standpoint.

Here are some examples of the types of questions economists would study depending on which of these two categories they are researching.

MICROECONOMICS

- Why did the consumer pick product A instead of product B?
- How does the supply of a product impact the demand for that product?
- How does a company determine what price to charge for its product or service?
- Why does job A have a higher salary than job B?

ALBAÑIL
LOSETA
DETALLES
DE YESO
RESANES
PINTURA

ALBAÑ
AZULEJO
LOZETA
RESANE

MACROECONOMICS

- Why is there so much unemployment across the country?
- How do the net imports as well as the net exports for the country affect jobs?
- What is the current rate of inflation?
- How healthy is the Gross National Product?

GROSS NATIONAL PRODUCT COMPARED TO GROSS DOMESTIC PRODUCT

The gross national product (GNP) is the total value of all the products and services offered by a particular country's citizens and their businesses. The GNP counts these values regardless of the location that the goods or services are produced. The GNP is the best measure of the income of all United States citizens. The United States has the highest GNP in the world.

The "health" of the United States economy is better measured by the gross domestic product (GDP). The GDP measures all the production that takes place in the United States even if the owners of a business are from foreign countries. For example, let's say the Toyota car company opens a plant in the state of Kentucky.

The profit from their sales goes back to Toyota, which is a Japanese company, but their work still helps the US economy because they are hiring and paying workers in Kentucky. The United States has the highest GDP in the world, about 25% of the world's total GDP.

SUPPLY AND DEMAND

In countries where the economy can be described as "free market" there is a natural balance of supply and demand. "Supply" simply means the amount of a particular product or item that is for sale at a given price and at a given time. "Demand" simply means the amount of a particular product that people wish to purchase at a certain price and also at a certain time.

With the volume set to "10," my tunes thump the bass in my headphones as I look up the lyrics with TuneWiki. 'Cause even a future rock star like myself needs help with the words.

my
Touch 3G

$199.99

Supply and demand go hand in hand with each other and they naturally adjust. Suppose you have a new electronic gadget to sell. If you produce lots of your gadget and the demand for it is the same as it was

before, the price will have to be adjusted down to get people to buy it. In other words, increased supply with demand the same, means that to sell them you may have to adjust prices down.

If you don't produce as many of your gadget, but the demand for it stays the same as it was before, the price will naturally adjust up since there are less of them to sell, but demand hasn't changed. In other words, decreased supply with demand the same, means that when selling them you may be able to adjust prices up.

If you produce the same amount of gadgets, but demand for them goes up, then the price will adjust up. In other words, if your production of gadgets hasn't changed, but suddenly the demand increases, you may be able to charge more.

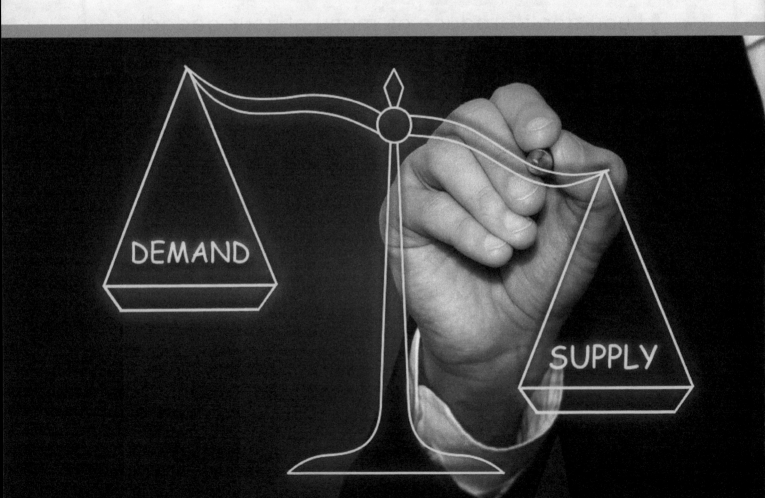

If you produce the same amount of gadgets, but demand for them goes down, the price will go down too. In other words, if your production of gadgets hasn't changed, but suddenly the demand decreases, you may have to lower your price to sell them.

GOODS AND SERVICES

There are two ways that businesses and individuals can make money. They can offer goods for sale or services for sale or a combination of both. For example, if you are the owner of a clothing store, you sell clothes and accessories.

These are items that people can pick up and look at before they decide to buy them. Any type of item that is a physical product falls into the category of "goods." Of course, you can also buy these types of goods online after seeing a picture of them.

As the owner, you decide that you also want to offer a service to your customers. You will tailor their suits for them as well. This is a service you offer your customers because it takes special skills in sewing and altering, but it doesn't produce an end product.

Automobiles, food, home decor, furniture, clothing, electronics, and computers are all examples of goods.

Tax preparation, writing and editing, medical care, hairstyling, babysitting, and landscaping are all examples of services.

TYPES OF ECONOMIES

There are four major types of economies.

TRADITIONAL

In an economy that is described as traditional, things haven't changed for a long time. The economy might be based on bartering as well as trading. Many economies that are based on farming would be considered traditional. In these types of economies, children might do the same exact work as their parents.

MARKET, ALSO CALLED FREE MARKET

In this type of economy, people can choose to buy whatever they want without the government telling them what they must do. Companies can also create and sell whichever products and services they want to offer as long as what they are producing or selling is legal. Supply of the products and demand for the products is what controls most of the flow of buying and selling. The government doesn't control every transaction so there's open competition between companies.

PLANNED OR COMMAND

Some countries have governments that control their economy. The country's government specifies which types of goods can be created as well as the price set for them.

In a planned or command economy, the government also controls who will receive the profits once something is bought or sold. In this type of economy, the government has the reins on all of the major industries.

MIXED

Most economies in the world today can be described as mixed. They are combinations of a free market economy with some level of planned control by the government. Frequently, certain types of industries have more government controls than others.

GLOBAL ECONOMY

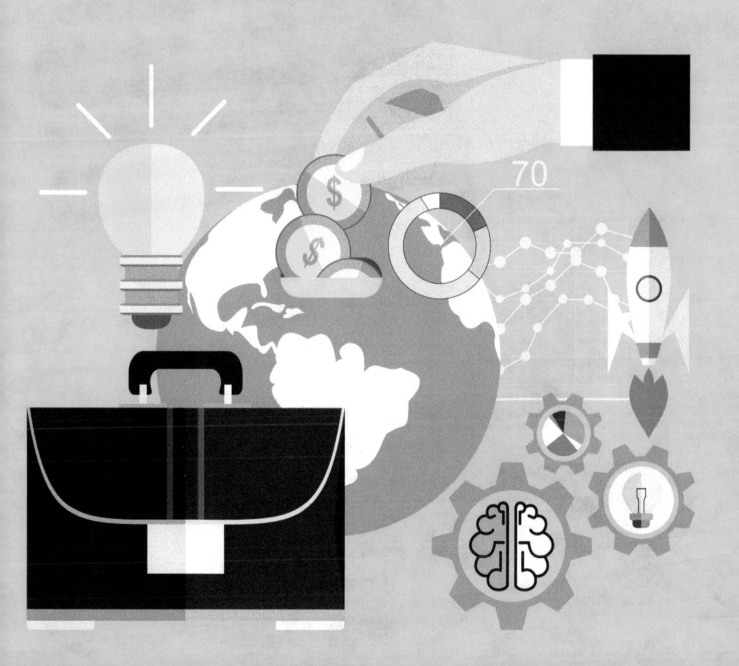

WHAT TYPE OF ECONOMY EXISTS IN THE UNITED STATES?

The economy of the United States is mostly a free market. However, the government does get involved in some regulations for how goods and services can be bought and sold.

For example, you can't sell goods without a valid resale certificate. Because there is some government regulation in the United States, the US economy would be considered a mixed economy.

Most countries today have a mixed blend of these different types of economies. However, in some countries, the government controls most aspects of how physical items and services are bought and sold.

IN CONCLUSION...

The economic conditions of a country give you a picture of its wealth as well as its resources. The way that goods as well as services are offered and priced is part of the economy. A good economy means that the people have jobs and that businesses are making a profit. Countries with poor economies don't have many jobs available and their businesses are losing money or are closing. Economic growth is important so that people can continue to improve their lives.

Awesome! Now that you've read about the economy, you may want to read more about money in the Baby Professor book Why Do We Need Money?

Visit

BABY PROFESSOR
EDUCATION KIDS

www.BabyProfessorBooks.com

to download Free Baby Professor eBooks
and view our catalog of new and exciting
Children's Books

CPSIA information can be obtained
at www.ICGtesting.com
Printed in the USA
BVHW090334100622
639230BV00007B/583